A Gracious Welcome

A Gracious Welcome

Etiquette and Ideas for Entertaining Houseguests

By AMY NEBENS

Photographs by Sang An
Prop styling by Philippa Brathwaite

CHRONICLE BOOKS

SAN FRANCISCO

Text copyright © 2004
by Amy Nebens.

Photographs © 2004
by Sang An.

Library of Congress Cataloging-
in-Publication Data available.

ISBN 0-8118-4083-2

Manufactured in Hong Kong

Prop styling by
Philippa Brathwaite

Food styling by Toni Brogan
Designed by Public

Distributed in Canada by
Raincoast Books
9050 Shaughnessy Street
Vancouver, British Columbia
V6P 6E5

10 9 8 7 6 5 4 3 2 1

Chronicle Books LLC
85 Second Street
San Francisco, California 94105

www.chroniclebooks.com

This book is intended as a practical guide to home decor crafts. As with any craft project, it is important that all the instructions are followed carefully, as failure to do so could result in injury. Every effort has been made to present the information in this book in a clear, complete, and accurate manner; however, not every situation can be anticipated, and there can be no substitute for common sense. Check product labels, for example, to make sure that the materials you use are safe and nontoxic. Be careful when handling dangerous objects. The author and Chronicle Books disclaim any and all liability resulting from injuries or damage caused during the production or use of the crafts discussed in this book.

Monopoly is a registered trademark of Hasbro. Scrabble is a registered trademark. All intellectual property rights in and to the game are owned in the U.S.A. and Canada by Hasbro Inc., and throughout the rest of the world by J.W. Spear & Sons Limited of Maidenhead, Berkshire, England, a subsidiary of Mattel Inc. Mattel and Spear are not affiliated with Hasbro.

Photographer's Acknowledgments

I would like to thank my assistants Yun Hee Kim and Adam Gardiner for all their hard work and support; prop stylist Philippa Brathwaite and food stylist Toni Brogan for their vision; my rep, Mary Dail for all her efforts; and Amy Nebens for the wonderful opportunity.

— Sang An

DEDICATION

To my loving husband, Edward, who is my biggest cheer-leader and my patient, first-line editor. To my beautiful children, who are my inspiration each and every day. And to my parents and sister, whose gracious styles have always shown me that anything is possible.

ACKNOWLEDGMENTS

This book was a collaboration by a wonderful group of people whose talent, insight, ideas, and dedication made it all possible. First my gratitude goes to Lisa Campbell, my amazing editor, for dreaming up this idea and allowing me to bring it to life—and for her constant guidance and encouragement along the way. I also want to thank photographer Sang An whose genius behind the camera brought visual beauty to the words. And prop stylist Philippa Brathwaite, who worked magic to show that details really do matter, and food stylist Toni Brogan, who turned simple recipes into works of art. Thanks also to the folks behind the scenes at Chronicle Books, who took the words and photographs and magically transformed them into this book: Jan Hughes, Doug Ogan, Vanessa Dina, and Steve Kim.

I would also like to acknowledge the generosity and kindness of family and friends who shared parts of their lives to help make this book happen. My sister and brother-in-law Joy and Morey Wildes who offered loving support and countless hours of expert advice. Barbara and Andrew Brill who selflessly allowed us to shoot in their beautiful home. Iris Kaplan, my mother, for her bountiful and delicious recipes. Irene Nebens, my mother-in-law, for equally tasty recipes, unending help in the kitchen, and for putting her sewing skills to work. Amy Conway for her ear and advice and her mother, Pat Hammond, for her delightful recipes, and Gabrielle Simon for her yummy recipes and unparalleled sporting knowledge.

Contents

INTRODUCTION

One of the most wonderful parts of making a home is inviting family and friends to share it, especially when plans call for them to stay overnight. For as guests ease into your daily routine, there is the luxury of time: conversations are not rushed, stories are not spared, and company is, quite simply, savored. If all goes well, these moments appear to unfold without effort. But as anyone who has ever entertained knows, that is not the case at all—success comes from the right mix of planning and preparing, ingenuity and spontaneity. These are well balanced by a host who knows how to make her guests feel at home: by creating a warm and comfortable environment and giving details their due. For two or for ten, entertaining houseguests is easier than you might think. And even if you don't have a lot of time on your hands, you can still infuse a wonderful sense of style into everything you do. Just relax, keep plans simple, and remember to enjoy yourself—that's the surest way that your guests will too.

The purpose of this book is to simplify the art of entertaining overnight guests by demonstrating how easy and fun it can be. It is for anyone, especially those who have the means for the first time—be it the space, the budget, or a free weekend—who wants to spend time with their favorite people in the comfort of their own home. You will see how to ready a space for guests, whether in a guest house, converted sewing room, or comfortable sleeper sofa in the den. You will also learn what to consider when organizing time spent with visitors—such as activities in your home or out and about—as well as meals. Here you will find simple, easy-to-follow recipes and suggestions of what could be store-bought instead for those busy days when a quick dinner-to-go is best. To that end, there are loads of time- and budget-saving tips that will still make it seem like you splurged. Look for decorating ideas, simple craft projects, and little details for personal attention, all of which impart the warmth and happy feelings that a gathering like this should bring.

The following pages are filled with practical information and advice, strategies, rules of etiquette, historical tidbits, and creative suggestions, as well as helpful tips and techniques, recipes, and project how-tos so you can make it all happen. Borrow the ideas you find in this book just as they appear or tailor them to meet your specific needs. In these busy times, when spending time is often limited to e-mails and phone calls, the hope is to inspire you to make room, literally and figuratively, for yourself and those who matter most. So plan your first housewarming weekend, set up space for out-of-town relatives, or start getting ready for that long overdue weekend with friends you haven't seen in ages. Let this book guide you, assist you, and help spark some wonderful ideas of your own.

Then, when the doorbells rings, take comfort that the flutter in your belly is the same that hosts have felt for centuries, all over the world. And know that in your tiny corner, you've created a haven for yourself and your guests, be it as humble as a soft embrace or as extravagant as a raucous jamboree. It will reflect you and your wish for happy memories to be made. So enjoy it all—the planning, the preparing, and the company—in your own gracious way.

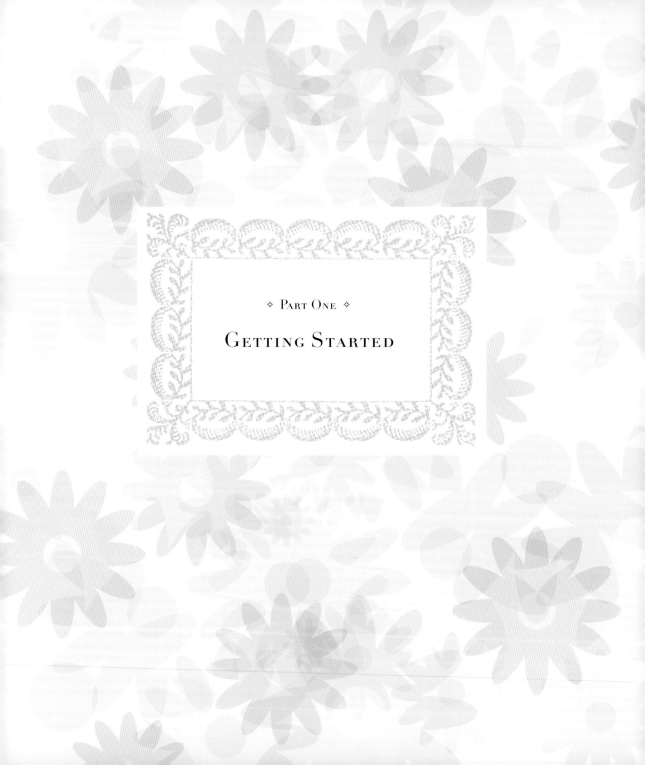

✦ Part One ✦

Getting Started

A house full of guests can feel like the most enchanted place on earth. Whether your parents are in town, your nieces and nephews are coming to stay (their first trip without their parents), or your very best friend from childhood has flown in for a whirlwind weekend, your home is immediately transformed. Lively moments filled with spirited conversations and hearty laughter easily fall into quieter ones—and back again. As host, you need to step away from time to time and tend to the duties at hand. Knowing just what those are and what is expected of you makes your job as simple and relaxed as it should be, and promises the most enjoyable time for all.

The reasons for entertaining are many, from holiday visits and family occasions, to social time with friends, to business functions. You and your college roommate who are now on opposite coasts may plan a weekend get-together during a graduate school vacation—and it may be the very first time either one of you has space enough to accommodate a guest and the other enough money to travel. Times like this typically call for a casual approach, but making all guests feel comfortable is still an utmost priority. Family weddings can double as family reunions, both at the festivities and at home. In this case, you will want to ensure that your relatives have plenty of social time to catch up and share photos and stories.

It's not necessary to be a seasoned host to create the perfect setting for these or any other visit. In fact, if this is the first time you've welcomed overnight guests, you likely already have an entertaining style even if you don't know it yet. Remember a weekend spent tucked into a quaint country inn and think about what struck your fancy and what didn't. Or what customs from your childhood home you have incorporated into your own. Think of your delight in choosing fresh flowers at a roadside stand and the joy you get from arranging them for your bedroom night table.

THE ROLE OF HOST

No matter who is coming, your responsibilities will begin well before your guests arrive and linger after they leave. This fact is not meant to deter you, just to help get you and your place in shape so that doing so does not feel tedious but as effort well spent. Map out plans clearly and handle what you can early on so you won't be overwhelmed or overburdened when guests do arrive—you will want to make the most of your time with them. There are certain standard practices you will want to follow, while specifics will be dictated by who is coming: your sister's children may be (as most are) particular about food, nap time, and activities; older guests, like your grandparents or an aunt or uncle, may not be as freewheeling as the younger set; your good friends may be thrilled to sit around chatting all weekend, while your brother and his buddies want to be shown the sights.

Of all the duties that make up the job of host, perhaps the most important is anticipating guests' needs so they feel as comfortable in your home as they would in their own. That said, no single aspect impacts a gathering as much as the right combination of many: a diverse and friendly guest list, timely invitations, cozy room assignments, delicious menus, organized activities, flowing schedules, and synchronized transportation. The actual space you make for others—in the bedrooms, bathrooms, living areas, and kitchen—should wrap them in comfort, delight them with details, and charm them with style.

Where to Begin

Planning starts the moment the idea for a gathering is born. First, the basics. Decide on a guest list, issue invitations, set up sleeping spaces, plan menus, arrange activities and transportation. Stay organized from the start. Keep a notebook, make checklists, then mark off tasks as you complete them. Next, focus on details, be they eminently practical points (providing directions back to your home from a few different points for guests setting out on their own) or gestures that go beyond what's necessary (appointing a guest room desk with picture postcards or sleek stationery, a good writing pen, and stamps). In the end, attention to these sorts of details is what truly makes a difference.

Don't assume plans need to be expensive; the best never are. It is your efforts—and the results, of course—that will be most appreciated and put guests at ease. Make planning simple now and in the future by having a regular repertoire of meals, plans, and activities, and then adding particular niceties to suit the people and the occasion. Rely on favorite stew recipes for winter and barbeque sauces for summer, then add seasonal dishes like fruit sorbets or potatoes au gratin and drinks depending on the time of year. Keep a collection of classic books and introduce other subjects depending on the crowd: political subjects are always fodder for interesting conversation and debate; biographies and comedic material provide plenty of entertainment. Have a stash of games for adults and toys for kids. Buy or make a guest book and leave it on an entry or living room table so guests can write messages at their leisure (see how to make a book, page 35). Be sensible and be creative—nothing needs to be perfect, just warm, stylish, and fun.

What Is Expected of You— and of Your Guests

A combination of the ideas from this book, your experience, and your instincts can make a visit with overnight guests all you hope for. The etiquette of entertaining is also a useful resource—think less in terms of stuffy, old-fashioned directives and more in terms of a contemporary protocol to help guide host behavior. You will find these rules sprinkled throughout the book. Follow them as much or as little as you like. Adapt them to make them your own and transform them to work perfectly in your home. Some of these are long-honored traditions, woven into the tapestry of time—not only are they intriguing and useful, knowing them means you don't start from scratch; a rich history and generations before have already established successful patterns to follow.

In ancient Rome, aristocrats traveled to lavish country estates to spend days gaming, socializing, and feasting. The socially elite of Victorian England lived during a time when country house visits were commonplace. Men and women alike abided by a very strict code of etiquette and were well schooled in the duties of host and guest. They had to be, since travel was by horse and carriage and slow at best, so such visits, to make them worthwhile, would extend for weeks at a time.

Understanding proper guest behavior will help you gauge your own reactions to countless situations. It is customary, for instance, for a guest to bring a small hostess gift. When presented with one, be delighted and thankful and use it if possible during the visit. When your sister's future husband presents you with a lovely bouquet of flowers, for example, be sure to arrange and display the flowers as quickly as possible—the sooner you get them into water, the better for the bloom, and it will no doubt delight him to know how appreciative you are. Don't just unwrap the cool bamboo tray your favorite aunt brought, set it out right away as a serving plate for hors d'oeuvres.

Respond to helpful requests, like assistance with cooking or cleaning up, honestly. If you and your best friend would like to steal a few minutes by yourselves from a big crowd, let her help in the kitchen while you're chopping vegetables. But, if you would rather work on your own, it's perfectly fine to say so. Be amenable to guests who propose activities. Nobody likes a bossy guest, but one who is a willing participant is always a pleasure.

Handle sticky situations, like a guest who plays music too loud or doesn't tidy up a shared bathroom, gently to avoid embarrassment—and remember this the next time you do the inviting. For a friend who has not mentioned transport to and from your home, either offer to pick him up or provide the names and phone numbers of local limousine and car rental companies. When your older brother asks to treat you to a night out, it says nothing about your cooking style. Accept his way of thanking you for entertaining him and enjoy the meal. A note written after guests arrive home to express gratitude for your hospitality is a pleasure to receive; no reply is necessary.

CREATING A GUEST LIST

If you are inviting just one person, a couple, or a family, you have a ready-made guest list. But if you will be hosting two or more people who are not necessarily connected, the guest list will establish the mood of the gathering, so make this your first task and give it careful consideration. The mix of people is crucial to your plans. If you are planning a big get-together, invite couples and singles, men and women, old and young—concentrating on interests and personalities. For a family-only guest list, think about who gets along best. When mixing special groups, consider who will likely come to your home as strangers and leave as friends. If there is someone who does not top your list but whom you have decided to include, don't second-guess yourself. Instead, look forward to spending time with this person and getting to know him or her in a different way.

If you don't entertain frequently, you might try to toss everyone you would like to see in together. As tempting as that may be, try to resist. Otherwise you may end up with former couples under the same roof along with new loves in tow — which may or may not be okay. Or family members who are just barely civil to each other. If it turns out you simply cannot avoid a sticky situation without insulting someone, let all involved parties know who is being invited. Then let them make the decision whether they will come or not.

Inviting children can be a sensitive area too. That's not to say children don't bring life to a party, because certainly they do. But catering to them will surely shift the focus of a weekend. You won't want to plan formal dinners, museum treks, and the like — rather, you'll be having fun with barbeques, parks, and group games. Surely guests without children should be welcome, but they might prefer to come instead when there will be an adults-only crowd.

EXTENDING INVITATIONS

Invitations give guests the first glimpse of your entertaining style. Think of what impression you'd like to make and what will be most appealing to those you are inviting. Telephoning is perfectly acceptable and, in fact, most typical. It is quick and easy and makes so much sense given today's hectic schedules. Be sure that when you call your mother-in-law to invite her for a weekend, you have your calendar in front of you so you can easily flip to an alternative if your first choice does not work for her.

As for e-mail, some find invitations made this way impersonal, others a hip and forward-thinking approach as well as convenient and time-saving. For many, e-mail is their main form of communication—and who wouldn't love to find a message reading "Come spend a few days at our house" among a bunch of business memos and unsolicited mail? You don't even need to be the one to initiate it. If a former colleague e-mails you to say she'll be in town for a night or two, respond right back and ask her to stay with you. E-mail specifics back and forth or call to finalize.

Invitations by post may be more formal or creative, depending upon the technique you choose. If you have the time and desire, they can be a lot of fun to make. A printed card sets the tone for a special occasion; a themed invite hints at the event to come. Kick off a bridal shower weekend with a favorite black-and-white photo of the bride; glue it to card stock and overlay with vellum paper that's been printed with all the information guests need to know. Invitations can also reflect the season: a stack of paper leaves in autumnal colors can be printed with details about a fall weekend in the country and bound by decorative ribbon. Pressed flowers are perfect for a festive weekend in spring. Pack them in a small glassine envelope with a card detailing the specifics. Or craft a card with a house motif (see page 25). A handwritten note is the most personal of all.

Unless it's a last-minute get-together, invitations should be made with plenty of notice—a month in advance, or even earlier if you are planning the visit during a holiday or with people who need to make airline or other travel reservations. If you have not received a response, follow up with a phone call at least two weeks before to leave plenty of time to prepare accordingly or to invite others you had originally hoped to but were not able to accommodate.

State Specifics

As host, you will establish when the visit will begin and end. Be clear about dates and timing in conversations and include it all in e-mails and cards. The more explicit you are, the better—it will take the guesswork out of many factors. People don't want to arrive too early or too late; they can figure out if there will be a meal or if they should eat before they arrive; and they will know what the attire will be. It is perfectly okay to say, "The weekend will begin with cocktails at seven o'clock on Friday, and end at two o'clock on Sunday—lunch will be served."

Be strategic in your scheduling: allow for plenty of travel time to your home so guests coming from a distance or after work will not miss out and, on their return, will reach home at a reasonable hour. Be mindful of mealtimes as well—travel can work up a hearty appetite. Victorian hostesses, ever attentive to their guests' well-being, would call for a late-afternoon arrival in order for people to have ample time to freshen up and dress for dinner.

If your guests will be driving, send them directions and an area map. Otherwise gather and send out train, bus, and ferry schedules; provide the name of the closest airport and airlines servicing it, if necessary. Local taxi and limousine service numbers always prove helpful, especially when multiple guests will be arriving from and into different locations. When your house will be the family hotel for an in-town wedding, bar mitzvah, or holiday celebration, surely you won't be able to make all the pickups and drop-offs, but when possible attempt to do so. It makes for a warm welcome from the start. Says *The Essential Handbook of Victorian Etiquette* (1873), "Have a carriage meet arriving guests. A family member with the carriage will make the welcome more pleasant."

Sleeping Arrangements

Whether you are entertaining in a vacation home, in a guest house, a guest room, or on a makeshift bed on a sofa, no space is too big or too small; the physical qualifications are quite limitless, really, as long as you've got enough room to provide accommodations for day and night.

Start with logistics: Everyone should fit comfortably in your home. Be sure there are enough beds for all. Do not include your bed in the count; guests will likely prefer the sofa than putting you out. Unless, of course, your sister or best friend is in town and the two of you will be tucked under the covers talking all night anyway. In this case, showing her to another room would be an insult—or pointless indeed. Do include your children's beds—your kids will likely be eager to give up theirs to a friend, aunt, or other guest for a chance to spend the night on the sofa or family room floor in front of the television. Also consider convertible sofas and roll-away beds; chosen right, both can be comfortable and easy to store. Air mattresses (invest in high-quality ones) are appropriate for the young and the limber, who can easily bend down to get into bed and hoist themselves from a low position to get up.

The downside of extra beds is that fitting them in usually means guests sharing rooms. Some people might not mind, while others might. Since the last thing you want to do is make anyone uncomfortable, avoid uneasy feelings by alerting people ahead of time if they will be expected to double up. If you sense any funny reactions, you'll have time to rethink arrangements. Married couples certainly expect to sleep two to a room but might not take kindly to the idea of additional roommates other than their own children. Older kids, though, like bunking separately from their parents, and vice versa, if you can spare the room. And maybe you can: children are the only exception to the one-bed-per-person (or couple) rule since they consider hunkering down in sleeping bags on the floor to be an adventure—ask them to bring their own if necessary (see page 39 for guest room specifics).

Invitation with House Motif

THE SIMPLE IMAGE OF A HOUSE IS THE ONLY ADORNMENT
NECESSARY ON A HANDMADE INVITATION. ANY WELCOME-
MOTIF APPLIQUÉ CAN BE USED SUCH AS A PINEAPPLE,
A BOUQUET OF FLOWERS, OR A SEASONAL ICON.

You will need:

*flat card stock or folded
invitation card, paper house
appliqué (available at craft
stores), glue (if using
nonadhesive appliqué)*

1. Handwrite or run card stock through computer to print
   pertinent information. Be sure printing is positioned so
   flat card can be folded.

2. Fold card stock in half or lay already-folded invitation on
   work surface.

3. In center of front side, affix appliqué to card with glue if
   not self-adhesive; position so appliqué will hold flaps of
   card closed.

Preparing for Different Needs

Children

Readying for the arrival of children is the perfect assignment to get a head start on, especially if the kids coming are infants and toddlers. Many people travel with their own baby equipment—portable cribs, high chairs, activity mats, and the like—but others may not be able to. Ask your girlfriend with toddler twins whether you can provide any gear. Find out specific requirements each item needs to meet: age, safety, purpose. If you have children yourself, think about your own baby supplies, either currently in use or stored away. If you will be having a steady stream of visitors with small children—perhaps you are a grandparent blessed with grandchildren—buying a few key pieces may make sense. If not, inquire at your local baby store about rental services or ask friends who are parents if they know of any. Send your friend a list of what you have and what you can and cannot get. You will also want to investigate baby-proofing—especially when there will be toddlers in town. It's amazing how quickly one little person can get into trouble on the stairs, in a cabinet, or simply by toddling, unseen, out the back door. Certain points may be obvious, like moving glass knickknacks to high shelves and household cleaners out of reach. If this is an area unfamiliar to you, ask the parents for suggestions.

Older children take some tending to as well. Out of their element, many demonstrate their wild side, especially when they are thrown into close quarters with cousins or friends they may not have seen in a long time. When five boys and three girls between the ages of two and ten will be around, don't anticipate a mellow visit or you will be sorely disappointed. While you can expect parents to keep some control over feisty moments, planning well will also help. When possible, invite families with children of similar ages. This way they can easily interact with each other and outings can be specially suited to them. For times when everyone is at home, have games and videos on hand and other activities thought out.

Children's attention spans are limited, so it helps to have a few things you can suggest at a moment's notice: puzzles, books, crayons and drawing paper, computer games, a park with play equipment down the block. Make children feel truly welcome by personalizing their stuff. For example, craft "journals" out of coloring paper just for them, then wrap a few colored pencils with twine to complete the presentation and give each kid his or her own set (see page 30). Other particulars, like feet muddy from outdoor play, for instance, can be easily and quickly remedied. Leave mats and wood boxes for shoes outside the front door and a kindly worded note reminding everyone to PLEASE REMOVE DIRTY SHOES.

Older Guests

Other guests whose requirements need to be specially considered include older folks who may not easily navigate stairways. Your instinct to treat your grandparents to the prettiest upstairs room will have to give in to good sense. If you can, accommodate them in a bedroom or elsewhere on the ground floor. Decorate their space with plenty of feel-good details—like pictures of you and your family, the most comfortable pillows and blankets, and favorite books or music you think they would enjoy—and they will feel like they are in the grandest space of all. Ask ahead of time if there is any way to make them more comfortable—for example, if a shower stall would be easier to maneuver than a tub where they will have to climb over a high side, or if a shower seat would make bathing simpler.

Health Issues

Consider everyone's state of health. Your brother with his well-known bad back will appreciate a good, firm bed rather than the sofa. Certain foods are off-limits for pregnant women, as is cigarette smoke. Downplay exotic dishes on menus and remind other guests to please refrain from smoking indoors. The last thing you need is your newly expectant sister-in-law holed up in her room all weekend or sending out for food. Guests with allergies often run into problems, some of which are unavoidable. Still, when aware of a potential situation, do what you can to rectify it. Move an outdoor barbecue inside when your husband's pal is overcome by tree and pollen allergies. Put off a trip to a riding stable to another day if your little nephew who can't come within a mile of a farm will have to stay behind.

CHILD'S JOURNAL AND PENCILS

IF YOU WILL BE HAVING MORE THAN
ONE YOUNG GUEST, MAKE THESE BOOKS WITH
COVERS IN EACH CHILD'S FAVORITE COLOR
(CALL THEIR PARENTS TO FIND OUT).

You will need:

scissors, ruler, pencil, about 20 sheets of 8$\frac{1}{2}$-by-11-inch construction paper (multicolored or single color), 1 sheet of 8$\frac{1}{2}$-by-11-inch construction paper in complementary color, 2 sheets of 8$\frac{1}{2}$-by-11-inch faux-wood cover paper or other decorative paper, 1 piece of 8$\frac{1}{2}$-by-11-inch card stock, hole punch, ribbon, glue stick, 5 or 6 colored pencils, twine

1. Trim construction paper into 8-by-8-inch squares. Cut cover papers to same size. Cut complementary piece of construction paper into 5-by-5-inch square. Cut card stock into 3-by-3-inch square.

2. Make stack of papers with cover papers on top and bottom and sheets of construction paper in between. On one side of the resulting square, punch 2 holes, $\frac{1}{2}$ inch from edge and 1$\frac{1}{2}$ inches from top and bottom. Thread ribbon through holes and secure in back with bow or knot. Trim ends. (Ribbon-bound edge will be left side of journal.)

3. Center 5-by-5-inch square on cover; glue in place. Sketch animal face, geometric shape, or child-friendly icon onto piece of card stock using a colored pencil. Center card stock on square and glue in place.

4. Bind colored pencils with twine and present with journal.

WELCOMING YOUR GUESTS

Include everyone in your welcome plan, whether you greet them at the door with a hug and a kiss, leave a handwritten note on their pillow, or place a welcome basket on their bedside table or bureau. A welcome basket can be arranged in an actual basket, galvanized bucket, wood box, or other roomy container. Include a note, itinerary (if applicable), activity suggestions, warm socks for the winter or sunscreen for the summer. A disposable camera is a good idea any time of year—dress it up in a smart felt cover (it's one of those simple-to-do but delightful details; see page 95). You may also want to pack a small gift—something of local flavor like maple syrup if you're in Vermont or a collection of beautiful seashells if you're by a shore—unless you want to save such tokens as a send-off gift. Either way, the favor will be a lovely reminder of their stay.

GUEST BOOK

A STORE-BOUGHT BOOK CAN BE PERSONALIZED OR, IF YOU
HAVE THE TIME, YOU CAN MAKE A GUEST BOOK YOURSELF.
THIS IS A PHOTO ALBUM AND GUEST BOOK IN ONE.

1. Take instant photos of guests when they arrive. Write
   their name and the date on the picture border.

2. Cut paper into 8-inch-wide strips, then score every
   8-inch length with bone folder to create accordion folds.

3. Tape lengths of paper together with paper tape until the
   "book" is as long as you like.

4. Center photos (1 to a page) about 1 inch down from top
   edge of page so there is plenty of room left to write a
   message; mark position lightly at corners with pencil.

5. Put photo corners in place and slip pictures in. Set
   guest book out on an entry hall table, in the living room
   on a side table, or elsewhere. Guests will look for their
   picture when they go to sign the book.

You will need:

*instant camera and film,
permanent marker with
a thin tip, thick paper, a
bone folder (a plastic tool
used to score paper), paper
tape or regular tape,
pencil, and photo corners*

◇ Part Two ◇

Preparing your Home

The physical aspect to entertaining is as important as the emotional. There needs to be adequate room for guests to sit, sleep, eat, play, and more. While most of the year your home is planned and decorated to suit your family's needs and interests, when overnight guests are coming, you'll want to make certain adjustments to meet theirs. Study every room, every nook and corner in your home—chances are you can make most spaces even more comfortable and inviting for visitors. Consider, for instance, a plump sofa in the den. Perhaps you can add a selection of books and magazines within easy reach and a light throw for cover. Stock guest bathrooms with essentials, in case guests forget theirs,

FLOWERS

Fresh flowers are one of the most important elements of gracious hospitality: they brighten a room, introduce a lovely, fresh scent, and show your attention to detail. Look for blooms in your garden, at a roadside stand or farmers' market, or at a local florist shop. There are so many possibilities; listed opposite are some organized by season, color, and fragrance to help you choose.

helpful items such as a sewing kit, a few pampering items like bath salts and candles. In guest rooms or those transformed into guest spaces, consider practical items, like a water carafe, an alarm clock, and extra blankets, as well as luxurious details like plush robes and slippers, fresh flowers, and herb sachets tucked into drawers (see page 48).

There is no need to spend a lot or to overthink this step— extravagant or unnecessary setups often seem out of place, can make guests feel ill at ease, and will leave you fraught and overwhelmed. Read on to find advice and ideas for almost every room of your home.

TAKING STOCK

Prepare your home as far in advance as you can. Less time fussing when guests arrive will leave more time for visiting— plus, you won't have any surprises wreaking havoc on your weekend. Make sure linens are laundered and ironed, bathrooms are spotless and in working order, and there are plenty of chairs for the dining table. The last thing you need is an out-of-commission guest toilet or running to the neighbors for folding chairs. Assess your supply of everyday plates, china, glassware, and flatware. Purchase whatever extra you will need, including paper goods. You'll want enough supplies for meals and snacks too. Polish and clean what needs it. Go over bar inventory—glassware, accessories, liquor, and mixers.

Your preparation will be dictated by the number of people coming and the activities planned—just be sure to think ahead and anticipate your guests' needs as well as your own: If your sister can't get by without a morning cup of coffee but you don't drink it, buy some freshly ground and purchase an inexpensive coffee maker. Or, if you know she is fine with instant, be sure to have some on hand. (See pages 74 to 86 for more details on food and drink.) If you're having Thanksgiving dinner at your home, in addition to six out-of-town relatives, do what you can well ahead of time so last-minute details don't take the fun out of the whole event.

Consider the season. During fall and winter months, clear room in your coat closet. Guests need easy access to their coats, umbrellas, and other cold-weather accessories as they come and go. Decide what outerwear your family will use during the visit and temporarily stow other items elsewhere. For warm-weather months, see that bicycles and other sporting equipment are in good shape and that storage sheds are cleaned out and easy to get into. Then you won't be worried about sending young children on a search for soccer balls or think twice when friends ask where you keep your tennis rackets. You will also want to give your house a thorough cleaning. It's also wise to tidy up your personal space, stowing any private items—from bank statements to prescriptions—out of view.

THE GUEST ROOM

A guest's room, whether a bedroom, transformed hobby room, or corner of the living room, is key to his or her comfort. From the moment they walk in your front door, it is the place to set down bags, settle in, regenerate after a long trip, take a snooze, escape from the crowd, and feel (temporarily) at home. For not only will guests be sleeping here, but they will also be napping, relaxing, visiting, primping, and dressing. Therefore, their room should be set up to meet all those needs and more. After you have spent your time and effort arranging as you

Flowers by Season

Most flower varieties are more beautiful and more abundant in their peak season. And since they don't have to be flown in from specialty nurseries or exotic locations, they will be less expensive than out-of-season blooms.

SPRING

bird of paradise, calla lily, dahlia, freesia, gardenia, larkspur, lilac, lily, pansy, ranunculus, rose, stephanotis, sweet pea, tulip, and zinnia

SUMMER

chrysanthemum, cosmos, delphinium, foxglove, gladiolus, hydrangea, iris, lily, peony, poppy, Queen Anne's lace, rose, snap-dragon, sunflower, tuberose

FALL

anemone, chrysanthemum, cosmos, gerbera daisy, hypericum (St. John's wort), iris, lily, orchid, pepper berry, rose, sunflower, zinnia

WINTER

amaryllis, aster, chrysanthemum, evergreens, gerbera daisy, holly, lily, narcissus

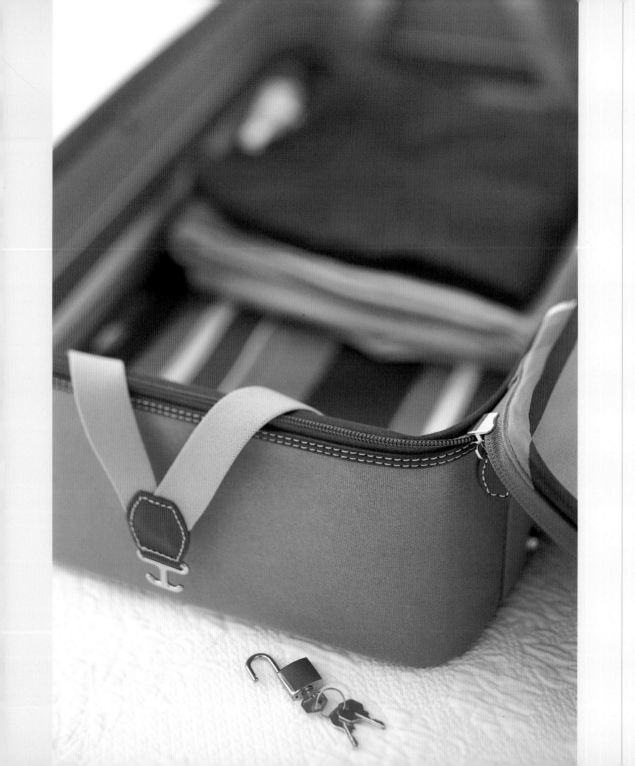

see fit, there is only one way to know it's all it should be: spend some waking hours in the room and sleep there overnight—only then will you truly see what it has, what is missing, what is wonderful, and what is not.

Every bedroom should have basics like empty drawer space so guests can unpack rather than living out of a suitcase. Clear out room in a bureau or dresser: for grown-ups, make space in top drawers so there is no need to bend; for children, lower drawers eliminate reaching on tiptoes. Put any items previously stored there in boxes or even a suitcase of your own and stash under your bed or in your closet for the duration. Clear off the top of the dresser or bureau and set with a stylish box or tray so guests have a convenient place to leave jewelry, wallets, watches, and the like. Leave empty hangers in a closet or armoire and relocate items you keep there so the closet is not overcrowded and maneuvering is manageable. On closet shelves, store a selection of extra blankets and pillows to meet varying guests' habits and preferences—a light throw for nap time, a heavy one for guests who get especially cold during the night, and a couple of pillows, one down-filled and one synthetic, if possible, for a guest with allergies.

Make the room a relaxing place to spend during the daytime, if your guest so chooses. Create a sitting area—so the bed is not the only place to sit down—where space permits. If you don't happen to have an extra wingback hanging around, use a spare dining room chair or even a comfortable folding chair set with a cushion and a small footstool.

Wonderful details give a room its charm and make it a comfortable place to be. The bedside stand is a good place to start. Bedsides an alarm clock, water carafe, reading lamp, and

Flowers by Color

Flowers in any hue are delightful, even more so when the shade complements the guest room or is your guest's favorite.

BLUE AND LAVENDER
anemone, delphinium, hyacinth, hydrangea, iris, lavender, lilac, lisianthus, muscari, rose, sweet pea, tulip

ORANGE
chrysanthemum, gerbera daisy, poppy, rose, tulip

PINK
anemone, astilbe, cherry blossom, cosmos, peony, rose, tulip

RED
amaryllis, dahlia, peony, ranunculus, rose, tulip, zinnia

WHITE
calla lily, chrysanthemum, delphinium, freesia, gerbera daisy, hyacinth, iris, peony, ranunculus, rose, snapdragon, sweet pea

YELLOW
calla lily, chrysanthemum, daffodil, dahlia, iris, lily, ranunculus, rose, snapdragon, sunflower, tulip, zinnia

Flowers by Fragrance

The scent of a flower can set a mood, conjure a memory, invigorate or relax. Choose your favorites or those you know your guests take a particular fancy to. Beware of putting strongly scented flowers in a bedroom or on a dining table. These are best in large common areas. Know too that scented foliage may affect those with allergies.

LIGHT FLORAL
bouvardia, carnation, chocolate cosmos, freesia, heliotrope, lily of the valley, rose, stock, sweet pea

HEAVY FLORAL
gardenia, honeysuckle, lilac, oriental lily, narcissus, some roses, stephanotis, tuberose

SCENTED FOLIAGE
dill, eucalyptus, lavender, lemon thyme, lemon verbena, rosemary

tissues, a bedside table should always have a fresh flower arrangement. Clip some blooms from your garden or go to a local farm stand or florist. How to choose? Go with your favorites, what's in season, or a choice you know would delight your guests. (Be aware, though, that heavily scented blooms may be too strong for some people.) If your parents are coming to stay and your mom's name is Iris or Rose, lucky you—it's an easy decision to make. Surprise your newly married friends with flowers just like the ones from their wedding. Change the water and clip the stems every day so the blossoms look fresh as long as possible. A stack of magazines and books will be much appreciated by anyone who wants to unwind before bed—popular mysteries, adventure stories, and biographies are good choices, and perhaps a volume on the meaning of dreams. You might also leave a pen and small journal for your guest to record the events of the day. If you like, provide a mini television and DVD or video player and a few films.

Have herbal teas and cocoas available in the evening. For the morning, consider the most indulgent detail of all: breakfast in bed. Set a tray with delectable breakfast food, like muffins (see page 77 for recipe) or scones (see page 79 for recipe), freshly squeezed orange or grapefruit juice, tea or coffee, a newspaper, and a pretty posy or two. Use a fine linen placemat and napkin for the most beautiful presentation.

If you don't have a designated guest room, you can certainly still have guests. Spare rooms—like a hobby room, home office, or exercise room—can easily be transformed. Where possible, move furniture or other equipment out of the center of the room to make space and put personal items, papers, and such away, out of sight. If you have a sofa bed already in the room, pull it out and make up the bed before guests arrive.

Nighttime Rituals

Treat your guests to some warm hospitality — attention to these fine points will make even the coldest nights warm.

- *While guests are just winding down their evening, go by each of their rooms and turn the light on — dimming it if possible. This way, rather than coming into a dark room, they will enter a warm, cozy space.*

- *Turn down the beds and fluff the pillows. Leave a handwritten note bidding them goodnight — or take it a step further and include tomorrow's forecast and a short outline of plans for the next day.*

- *Leave a tasty piece of chocolate, a mint, or other indulgent sweet as a treat on the pillow. (To make the wrapping as special as what's inside, see page 51.)*

- *For young guests, especially those visiting without Mom and Dad, leave a couple of cookies and a glass of milk or cup of cocoa at their bedside. Little ones make instant pals with stuffed animals. Ask if they'd like to be tucked in, want a bedtime story, and prefer to sleep with their door open or closed and the hall light off or on.*

If not, make up a sofa, an air-mattress, or a roll-away bed. No matter where it is, a well-made bed immediately says "bedroom." Hang a guest robe and extra hangers from high bookshelves or on hooks on the back of the door if there is no room in the closet, or no closet at all. Make room for shoes beside the bed or under a window; let a bookshelf or side table become a nightstand.

If you live in an apartment and have no true "extra room," there are probably alternative spaces with which you can easily make do: a living room with a pullout sofa, an alcove with floor space for an air mattress, a dining area that can be screened off. Since such spaces are most likely to be used for different purposes during the day and night, it's best not to make up a bed in them until evening. When your mom comes for a visit to see your first home, you'll want to use the den to chat, relax, and hang out. Take the bed out only when she is ready for sleep. For a quick fix: leave sheets and blanket on, so you will only have to add pillows to the pulled-out bed. Or keep a basket handy with all the necessary items, from linens and pillows to a pair of slippers.

When possible, rooms for children should be made up just for them. Petite pillows and blankets are more inviting than adult-size gear. Kids' books are a welcome and familiar sight, as are coloring books and a stash of crayons and markers— get some with the latest pop characters and you'll be the new favorite auntie. Put a basket of playthings by the foot of the bed or in an easy-to-reach corner; fill it with age-appropriate toys and soft stuffed animals. For safety reasons, be sure all electrical outlets are covered and any cords or heavy objects well out of reach. For parents of visitors still in diapers, create a makeshift changing area, complete with a changing pad or towels, and stock it with disposable diapers (ask about the proper size), wipes (unscented is always best), petroleum jelly, diaper rash lotion, cornstarch powder, and a plastic bag–lined trash can with a lid.

If your guest is on a business trip or needs to study while staying with you, try to accommodate his or her needs with a writing surface, extra phone (a separate line is ideal), fax machine, plus writing supplies, paper clips, and so on. That's not to say you must rearrange the whole space or buy expensive equipment—just do what can easily be done. Type up instructions for using your computer when you're not home and identify the locations and pickup times of the nearest post office and private mail services.

GUEST-FRIENDLY ART

Turn useful information or incidental details into pretty decorations for guest rooms.

- *Take a detailed area map (or a historic one of your town) and put it in an inexpensive frame. Store or move existing art.*

- *Suspend a homemade paper cone filled with flowers and marked with guest's name on the door handle to personalize a room (see page 52).*

- *Display an array of beach bags or shopping totes (color coordinated, of course) on hooks on the back of a bedroom door or attach them with clothespins to a ribbon suspended along the inside of an armoire door.*

- *Make a montage of photos and place it on the bedside table—for family, use both old and new pictures. A few black-and-white shots of grandparents and great-grandparents make a lovely artistic state- ment and an especially meaningful one. For friends, combine group pictures and individual shots, including friends who are joining you and those who couldn't make it. Copy photos on copy*

(continued)

Guest Room Essentials

⋄ Alarm clock (with dual alarms for couples and families) ⋄

⋄ Telephone with list of local phone numbers
(recommended restaurants, stores, movie theaters,
hospital, police) and phone books ⋄

⋄ Water carafe and tumbler ⋄

⋄ Books ⋄

⋄ Full-length mirror ⋄

⋄ Daily newspaper with local section ⋄

⋄ Television and radio channel guide
(if there are a television and radio) ⋄

⋄ Starched linens — cotton or linen are best ⋄

⋄ Iron or steamer ⋄

⋄ Laundry bag (and access to your washing machine) ⋄

⋄ Blackout emergency kit
(candles, flashlight, battery-operated radio) ⋄

⋄ Nightlight, for trips to and from kitchen or bathroom
in unfamiliar surroundings ⋄

machine, trim some to shapes of silhouettes and leave others intact, then place in a frame. Take this approach rather than just a photo of you and your guest in a frame— if it's not already really displayed—or it might seem contrived instead of fun and sentimental.

- *In lieu of a bedside lamp, display a cluster of pillar or votive candles and light them for bedtime reading — these are also good to have on hand in the event of a blackout.*

- *Draw a simple map of a few-block radius of your home, marking off favorite places, if you live in a city where the gridlike layout is simple to render. This will make your favorite coffeehouse, park, and theater easy to find. Hang as room decor or give guests to take on outings.*

- *Frame black-and-white or color postcards of the area. Use postcards of historic scenes or ones that depict famous structures, buildings, or landmarks. Arrange on a wall, desk, or table.*

LAVENDER SACHETS

PLACE THESE PETITE PILLOWS, FILLED WITH THE RELAXING
HERB LAVENDER, IN DRAWERS OR UNDER PILLOWS FOR
A HIDDEN SOURCE OF FRAGRANCE.

**You will need for
each sachet:**

*sewing equipment, 2 pieces
of 5-by-5-inch fabric, 22
inches of rickrack or piping,
and 2 to 3 tablespoons of
dried lavender*

1. Place both pieces of fabric right side up; pin edges over
   $1/4$ inch to hide rough edges or serge the edges.

2. Place one fabric on top of the other so right sides face in.
   Pin together on 3 sides. If using rickrack or piping, lay
   along edges of bottom piece before placing top fabric on,
   so rickrack or piping edge faces in to center of fabric; sew
   as close to piping, if using, as possible. Place top fabric on
   and sew to secure. Fold trim corners neatly as you go
   around corners. Repeat on all sides.

3. Turn fabric right side out; spoon lavender into pocket,
   place trim in place, then stitch fourth side closed.

Wrapped Candy Box

A WHIMSICAL TAKE ON "TURN-DOWN CHOCOLATES,"
THESE SPECIALLY WRAPPED BOXES CAN BE FILLED WITH
ANY CANDY, SUCH AS COATED MINTS, CHOCOLATES, NUTS,
OR DRIED FRUIT.

1. Fill box with treats.

2. Measure paper to wrap box and cut.

3. Wrap box just as you would any present, taping folds
   in place to secure.

4. Tie ribbon around box.

5. Turn down blanket and sheets and set box at base
   of pillow.

You will need:

*small box, food treat,
decorative or wrapping
paper, scissors, tape,
and complementary
decorative ribbon*

HANGING DOOR SIGN

A CONSIDERATE WAY TO MAKE GUESTS FEEL AT HOME, ESPECIALLY WHEN YOU HAVE A LARGE GROUP, THIS INEXPENSIVE, EASY-TO-MAKE SIGN MARKS EACH GUEST'S ROOM AND CAN BE FILLED WITH FLOWERS FOR AN ESPECIALLY WELCOMING DETAIL.

You will need:

scissors or utility knife, vellum paper, computer and printer, colored card stock, hole punch, grosgrain ribbon in color a few shades darker than card stock, glue, flowers

1. Using computer, print guest name vertically on vellum, about 2 inches down from top edge and centered horizontally on sheet.

2. Cut vellum into 8-by-8-inch square and roll into a cone.

3. Cut card stock into 4-by-8-inch strip. Wrap around vellum cone, aligning bottom edges.

4. Using hole punch, punch hole at left and right sides of vellum, about $1/4$ inch from top.

5. Cut ribbon to 12-inch length; run ribbon through holes and tie ends in knots to secure.

6. Loop ribbon around door handle and let hang.

7. Fill with fresh or dried flowers.

The Guest Bath

The bathroom—whether guests will have their own or will be sharing—is a very personal space, so choose its contents and setup carefully. Appoint it with fundamentals and fit it with some extras, because no one should be without a bit of pampering. Different people will use the bathroom differently—your brothers-in-law (in fact, many men) will be in and out, taking care of basic needs quickly. Women, on the other hand, may spend more time there, washing, relaxing, and primping. You know your dad will take a quick shower, while your mom likes to luxuriate in a long, sudsy bath. It isn't always possible to meet everyone's particular needs and desires, but you can do your best. Make ample space, provide comfortable necessities, add a few indulgent luxuries, and you will be set.

Take a visual walk around your bathroom and consider what you need where: start with the tub, then move to the sink, the counter, the medicine chest. In the tub, you will need soap, shampoo, and conditioner (all new, of course) but don't fret about pleasing different tastes. Maybe choose one or two different products and leave it at that. Your girlfriend with the great highlights will likely bring her own supplies. Don't forget shower caps for those who may use them, and provide a clean bath towel, hand towel, and a couple of washcloths for each guest. Place a bath mat near the tub or shower.

On the counter or in a drawer, place an assortment of sundries (see list on page 59) and specialty items like mud masks and facial ingredients (see page 65 for a homemade recipe). Don't forget drinking glasses, magnifying mirror, and a hair dryer. Use this as an opportunity to clean out old or unused stuff. Buy inexpensive but chic containers for toner and lotion or apothecary jars for swabs and cotton balls.

Color-Coding

If you are having a big group to your home, a fun, decorative way to help guests keep track of items they're using is to color-code them: for each guest, provide items all in one specific shade or labeled with coordinating ribbons and tags. Some examples:

- *Rickrack sewn along the hems of white towel sets (see page 60)*
- *Ribbons sewn onto robe sleeves and slippers*
- *Different-colored towel sets*
- *Different-colored tumblers and toothbrushes*
- *Different-colored tags attached to lotions*
- *Different-colored tags tied to baskets or buckets for sundries*

Aromatherapy

You can buy items with essential oils such as soaps, shampoos, bath gels, bath salts, candles, lotions, and facial ingredients. Certain fragrances have powerful effects on our moods, desires, and energies. Here are some scents, their properties, and how you might put them to good use.

Invigorating Fragrances

Perfect before an activity-filled day of hiking, biking, or sightseeing or a night of celebrating and dancing at a wedding or reunion.

- *Clove*
- *Lemon*
- *Peppermint*
- *Rosemary*
- *Spruce*

Most guests will bring their own hygiene essentials, like their toothbrush, hairbrush, and comb, but it's always smart to keep some extras in the event they don't. If you like, pack items—those just mentioned, as well as a handheld mirror, bobby pins, soap and travel dish, and lip balm—in a zippered travel pouch and attach a gift tag with your guest's name, so she knows it's hers to use and take home.

Making Room

Depending on the size and layout of your home and your guest list, you may be able to put one guest to a bathroom or have a few share the same. No matter. All it takes is a little space and time management to give everyone privacy. If you can, set aside space in the linen closet, marking shelves with each guest's name for easy identification. On each shelf, place a selection of bath linens, a plush robe for cold weather or a light linen or waffle-weave style for spring and summer months, and comfortable slippers. If you don't have extra shelf space, fold these items neatly, tie with a ribbon, and leave on each guest's bed, with a note that reads FOR THE BATH.

If you've got one bathroom to share with a single guest, label an inexpensive wood crate, galvanized bucket, or wire basket with her name and place on the counter, a side table, or against the back wall so she can unpack personal items in the bathroom but remain in her own space. Do the same thing—in multiple—for a houseful of guests, like your oldest and dearest friends bunking with you the weekend of your high school reunion, who will be sharing a bathroom. Put some practical devices in place to ensure everybody's comfort and the room's accessibility. For privacy, perhaps an IN USE sign to post on the door and a sign-up sheet for showering.

SUNDRY CHECKLIST

⬦ Hand and face soap ⬦

⬦ Lotion ⬦

⬦ Toothbrushes ⬦

⬦ Toothpaste ⬦

⬦ Mouthwash ⬦

⬦ Dental floss ⬦

⬦ Disposable razors ⬦

⬦ Shaving cream ⬦

⬦ Tweezers ⬦

⬦ Cotton balls ⬦

⬦ Rubbing alcohol ⬦

⬦ Nail file and clipper ⬦

⬦ Lint brush ⬦

⬦ Antibiotic ointment ⬦

⬦ Acetaminophen
and aspirin ⬦

⬦ Antihistamine lotion
and pills ⬦

⬦ Adhesive bandages ⬦

⬦ Petroleum jelly ⬦

⬦ Sewing kit with a few basic
tools, thread, and buttons ⬦

Extras for the Bathtub

⬦ Loofah, sea sponge, or scrub brush ⬦

⬦ Terry wash mitt ⬦

⬦ Pumice stone ⬦

⬦ Bath pillow ⬦

⬦ Bath tray ⬦

⬦ Bath salt mix (see page 62) ⬦

⬦ Candles ⬦

Relaxing Fragrances

After a day on the go, sightseeing, hiking, and swimming, or a weekend of nonstop festivities and celebrations.

- *Chamomile*

- *Jasmine*

- *Lavender*

- *Rose*

Stress-Relief Fragrances

For parents, anyone in town on business, and active participants in weddings or a string of family events.

- *Nutmeg*

- *Orange*

- *Vanilla*

RICKRACK TOWELS

THIS PROJECT MAKES THE MOST IMPACT WHEN WHITE TOWELS ARE USED, BUT ANY COLOR TOWEL WILL DO, SO LONG AS THE RICKRACK SHOWS UP WELL.

You will need, for each set:

bath sheet or towel, hand towel, and washcloth in same color; measuring tape; rickrack trim in solid color; thread of same color; sewing supplies

1. Beginning with bath sheet or towel, lay flat and measure front bottom edge, from left to right. Measure rickrack to same length and cut.

2. Pin rickrack in place along hem of towel, lining up bottom, left, and right edges.

3. Sew trim in place along hem and secure on left and right sides. Repeat on hand towel and washcloth.

BATH SALT MIX

PAMPER YOUR GUESTS WITH A SOOTHING BATH TREAT THAT'S PERFECT FOR THE END OF AN ACTIVE DAY. LEAVE A TINY SPOON OR SCOOP BESIDE THE JAR OF SALTS SO GUESTS KNOW THEY ARE TO USE AND NOT SIMPLY FOR DISPLAY.

You will need:

bath salts in at least 4 colors (choose those that complement your bathroom's decorating scheme so you can leave out on display), decorative glass or plastic jar with lid, spoon

1. Wash and dry jar and lid; set aside.

2. Set out bath salts, divided by color.

3. To make bands of color, spoon enough of 1 color into jar to make wide band; do not pat down top of mound. Continue adding other colors in same way until jar is filled. To make speckled mixture, add 4 spoonfuls of 1 color to the jar, then 4 of another; shake gently to mix; repeat process with remaining 2 colors, then start again with the first, shaking gently to mix after each set of 4 spoonfuls.

At-Home Herbal Steam Facial

SISTERS, GIRLFRIENDS, AND MOMS WILL ALL APPRECIATE
THIS LUXURIOUS TREAT. MAKE A BEAUTIFUL PRESENTATION
THAT SMELLS AND FEELS GOOD TOO. CHOOSE HERBS (AVAIL-
ABLE AT HEALTH FOOD AND SPECIALTY STORES) THAT HAVE
RELAXING PROPERTIES FOR BEFORE BED OR WILL OFFER A
PICK-ME-UP IN THE MORNING OR BEFORE A NIGHT OUT.

1. Handwrite instructions for facial on a flat or tented card
   or print them out using a computer.

2. Set out for guests next to the bowl of herbs, face lotion,
   and a plush hand towel.

Herb facial instructions:

1. Fill sink or basin a quarter full with steaming hot water.
   Add herbs, then continue to fill sink with hot water until
   a little more than half full.

2. Pull hair back from face, drape towel over head to create a
   "tent," and lean over sink, close enough so that steam can
   penetrate pores, but not so close that skin feels too hot.

3. Breath in and out steadily, slowly, and deeply. Remain
   under "tent" 5 to 10 minutes.

4. Pat face dry with towel.

5. Apply your favorite face lotion.

You will need:

*Pen or computer
and printer, card stock,
attractive small bowl,
herbs for the recipe you
have chosen, face lotion,
hand towel*

Relaxing recipe:

*Combine $1/3$ cup lavender,
$1/3$ cup chamomile,
and $1/4$ cup rose petals*

Pick-me-up recipe:

*Combine $1/4$ cup peppermint
or $1/4$ cup rosemary, and
$1/4$ cup cloves*

THE LIVING AREA

Any living space in your home becomes a community space once guests arrive, whether a family room, living room, playroom, rec room, screened porch, or deck. The trick is to make it comfortable for everyone to enjoy at the same time. To do this, equip the space to suit many purposes: quiet time and social time, party time and play time. You will want to provide a variety of easily accessible books, magazines, board games, CDs, and videos or DVDs, plus a television and movie channel guide. Be sure there is enough to interest people of all ages. That's not to say that if you don't have children, you need to go out and buy a bunch of kids' tapes and books. Instead, if your sister is coming with her three kids, remind her to bring their favorites, or find out what they are and ask neighbors or nearby friends if you can borrow any from them.

Snacks for Socializing

The living space is also the best place for entertaining with cocktails and hors d'oeuvres, late-night snacks, and refreshments. If you are planning a cocktail hour, invite local friends to meet your relatives who live far away, and let family members know what time it's called for so they can clear out of the room to get themselves ready and leave you time to clean up, rearrange furniture, and set up for a crowd. For movie or game nights, place snacks in bowls, plates, and other containers and scatter them about the room — put mixed spiced nuts on the mantel; dips, vegetables, mini breads, and chips on the coffee table; and wait to bring out cookies and brownies until later in the evening. Place a table in a strategic location for any beverages you will serve, such as flavored iced teas (see pages 82–85), hot teas, and coffee. Be sure to have kid-friendly food and drink, as well as any specialty items to meet the dietary restrictions of your company.

STOCKING THE BAR

JUST WHAT LIQUOR, MIXERS, AND GARNISHES TO STOCK
WILL VARY WITH THE TYPE OF DRINKS YOU TYPICALLY SERVE
AND THOSE YOUR GUESTS LIKE TO DRINK. OF COURSE,
IF YOU WILL BE HOST FOR A PARTY OR DINNER,
KEEP EXTRA ON HAND.

Liquor	Mixers	Garnishes
Bourbon	Orange juice	Lemons, limes, and oranges (for wedges and zest)
Amaretto	Cranberry juice	
Brandy	Lemons and limes (for fresh juice)	Maraschino cherries
Baileys Irish Cream	Pineapple juice	Celery stalks
Gin	Grapefruit juice	Cocktail onions
Crème de cacao	Tomato juice	Olives
Rum (light, dark, spiced)	Sour mix	Strawberries
Grand Marnier, Triple Sec, or other orange-flavored liqueur	Bloody Mary mix	Heavy (whipping) cream (for whipping)
Scotch	Piña colada mix	Coarse salt
Tequila	Bitters	Sugar
Kahlúa	Grenadine	Cocoa powder
Vodka	Simple syrup	Nutmeg
Peach schnapps	Worcestershire sauce	
Whiskey	Tabasco sauce	
Sherry	Club soda or seltzer	
Red wine	Tonic	
Vermouth (sweet and dry)	Cola and diet cola	
White wine	Lemon-lime soda	
Champagne	Ginger ale	
	Heavy (whipping) cream or half-and-half	
	Milk	
	Crushed ice	
	Ice cubes	

MAKING ROOM TO SIT

When having a crowd, get creative and flexible with furniture and accessories to make enough seating space for everyone. Doing this might turn formal spaces into more casual and welcoming ones.

- *Move oversized throw pillows from the sofa to the floor.*

- *Move ottoman or other footstool away from intended chair to make its own seating spot.*

- *Bring dining chairs into the living room and pad with small pillows or chair pads.*

- *Consider taking (clean) lawn furniture inside, especially a free-standing covered swing or a bench — these seats usually have room for more than one.*

- *Set out blankets or throws for kids and make a picnic or play area for them right on the floor.*

Sangria

FOR A NONALCOHOLIC VERSION, SUBSTITUTE GINGER ALE
FOR THE BLUSH WINE. *Serves 12*

- *4 cups blush wine*
- *¼ cup sugar*
- *1 ounce freshly squeezed lemon juice*
- *2 cups seltzer*
- *1 orange, sliced into rounds*
- *6 strawberries, sliced (or more to taste)*
- *1 ripe peach, pitted and sliced*
- *2 long lemon peel twists*

1. Combine wine, sugar, lemon juice, and seltzer in large glass pitcher filled with ice; stir with wooden spoon until sugar has dissolved.

2. Add orange, strawberries, and peach slices and lemon peels; stir gently.

3. Serve in wineglasses.

Stamped Cocktail Napkins

HAVE A STAMP CUSTOM MADE WITH YOUR NAME, MONOGRAM, OR THE DATE OR FIND A PREMADE INITIAL OR MEANINGFUL SYMBOL AT ANY CRAFT OR STATIONERY STORE.

You will need:
plain paper cocktail napkins, rubber stamp with design of your choice (see headnote), ink pad.

(Note: it's always a good idea to do a couple of test stamps on scrap paper before using on napkins.)

1. Lay cocktail napkins one at a time on work surface.

2. Press rubber stamp lightly onto ink pad—you want intended design to be fully coated but not the outline of the physical stamp.

3. Position stamp carefully over napkin, centering design, aligning it with edges, or whatever you desire. Press down firmly for 5 seconds and carefully lift off.

4. Repeat on remaining napkins.

◆ Part Three ◆

Spending Time
with Guests

As soon as you've got your home in order, turn your attention to how you and your guests will spend time once they arrive—because isn't that the reason you are getting together in the first place? Mealtime can be quality time, as can day trips, short outings, and leisurely interludes spent hanging around your home. Plan as much as you can in advance—including menus and potential activities—so you won't be stuck shopping while everyone else is out having fun, or racking your brain for things to do.

Drinks and Snacks

Guests may get hungry between meals or just want something quick and easy to eat. Here are basics you will want to have on hand.

- *Water (still and sparkling)*
- *Soft drinks (regular and diet)*
- *Seltzer/tonic*
- *Fruit juices*
- *Milk*
- *Wine*
- *Coffee*
- *Tea (black and herbal)*
- *Chips, crackers, pretzels, popcorn, etc.*
- *Trail mix*
- *Mixed nuts*
- *Fresh fruit*
- *Fresh vegetables, washed and sliced*
- *Cheeses*
- *Cookies, brownies, biscotti, etc*
- *Sliced meats*
- *Bread*
- *Variety of dry and hot quick cereals*
- *Breakfast bars*
- *Peanut butter*
- *Jelly, jam, honey*

Mealtime

Meals are the first order of the day, and in some instances the last. Preparing for them does not have to be as daunting as it may sound. Plan menus early on and keep them simple. Prepare any dishes that can be made ahead and freeze or refrigerate. Choose prepared items at the store to complement homemade dishes and ease your workload. For added efficiency, consider what leftovers can be used as ingredients the following day, like a poached-salmon dinner entrée from Saturday night that can be tossed into a brunch salad on Sunday or a mixed-fruit appetizer that can be coated with brown sugar and baked as dessert for another meal (see page 76 for more ideas). Ask first-time visitors about any taboo foods and any favorites so you can steer clear of what you need to and delight them with the rest.

Make lunch and breakfast informal so no one feels bound by scheduled seatings. Morning may be bustling with activity as people head out the door to go this way or that—or it may be lazy for those who like to sleep in. Have a pot of coffee brewing and tea water warming for early risers, and set out a selection of teabags, juices, homemade muffins (see recipe on page 77), scones (see recipe on page 79), pastries, and fruit so they can help themselves. Check the supply and refill as necessary throughout the morning. Other, more substantial, breakfast options that are still easy include oatmeal, scrambled eggs, and toast. Set these out on a warming plate so guests can still serve themselves. Have flatware and napkins stacked or arranged in glasses and left out on the counter, so guests don't have to rummage through your cupboards to find what they need—for breakfast or at any time during the day.

Lunch can be a picnic packed in a basket or backpack for a hike or afternoon bike ride, a selection of finger foods poolside, or an assortment of salads, grilled vegetables, cheeses, and meats

Putting Leftovers to Good Use

To save time and money, turn one meal into two or three by using what's left from a lunch or dinner dish and transforming it into part of the next day's breakfast or lunch.

- *Salads can be made from almost anything: steak, fish, or chicken from dinner can easily become a gourmet salad the next day, warmed up or served chilled; a side of grilled or fresh vegetables are just as good when plated, drizzled with vinaigrette, and tossed with mixed greens; cold cuts from one lunch can be added to a chef's salad.*

- *What's fun about an omelet is to see just what's inside: leftover ham, sliced bell pepper, and cheese from a cheese-and-cracker platter all make for appetizing fillings.*

- *No matter the size of fruit salad you make, there always seems to be more in the bowl. To use up, coat the fruit with brown sugar and sauté in a pan with butter and a pinch or two of curry for a scrumptious dessert; freeze grapes and berries for refreshing snacks; make a creamy ambrosia salad sprinkled with chopped nuts; or add fruit juice and rum for a summer punch.*

set out buffet style with a basket of breads, including rolls, baguettes, and croissants to encourage sandwich making. Or give the spread a Mediterranean twist with hummus, baba ghanoush, and tabbouleh and plenty of pita or lavash on the side. Iced teas and lemonades are refreshing in spring and summer; hot cider and tea are wonderful for colder seasons. Always have plenty of water on hand—fill one pitcher with still water and another with sparkling and garnish with colorful slices of orange, lemon, and lime.

At country estates in nineteenth-century England, dinner was the day's main event. Follow this tradition, and your dinners will be a wonderful time for host and guests alike. Whether you and your guests spend the day together in town or scattered about at the beach, exploring nature trails, or soaking up local culture, expect to gather at the table to share news about the day, a meal, and an evening. Make the meal your activity—an outdoor barbecue or clambake can last well into the night—or schedule it early enough so it is only the beginning.

If you will be going to a restaurant, you will want to make reservations—especially for a large crowd. Since the bill is your responsibility, avoid discussion with guests who want to pay their share by making previous arrangements with the maître d' or manager. In some circumstances, a guest may ask to treat you; if you are comfortable with this, accept the offer gracefully. Whether dining at home or out, make guests aware of general plans before they arrive so they will know what to pack. Also, while they are at your home, tell them in advance what time dinner is called for. Give a gentle reminder half an hour or so before so they can change and get ready for the evening. After the meal, offer tea and coffee or a nightcap. When you are ready for sleep, wish your guests a good night, and encourage them to stay up as long as they wish.

Gab's Apple Muffins

MAKE THESE MUFFINS JUST BEFORE GUESTS ARRIVE—
THEY WILL FILL YOUR HOME WITH A YUMMY SMELL
AND STAY FRESH UP TO 2 DAYS WHEN COVERED. LIGHT
AND DELICIOUS, THEY'RE AN EASY SNACK FOR ANY
TIME OF DAY. *Makes 12 muffins*

1. Preheat oven to 400°F. Coat a 12-well muffin pan with cooking spray (or line with cupcake cups).

2. Sprinkle apples pieces with the 1 tablespoon flour.

3. In a large mixing bowl, combine all remaining dry ingredients, except brown sugar. Mix well.

4. In a separate bowl, mix the egg, brown sugar, butter, and yogurt. Incorporate into dry mixture.

5. Add the apples and mix until coated.

6. Spoon or pour mixture into prepared pan; fill each cup three-quarters full.

7. Bake 15 to 20 minutes, until golden brown (a toothpick inserted into the center of a muffin should come out clean when muffins are done).

8. Remove pan from oven and let cool about 5 minutes before removing muffins. Transfer muffins to a wire rack to cool 5 minutes more.

* *1 cup peeled and chopped Granny Smith apples*
* *2 cups, plus 1 tablespoon all-purpose flour*
* *1/2 teaspoon baking soda*
* *2 teaspoons baking powder*
* *1/2 teaspoon salt*
* *1 1/2 teaspoons cinnamon*
* *1/2 teaspoon nutmeg*
* *1 egg, lightly beaten*
* *1/2 cup firmly packed brown sugar*
* *1/2 stick (2 ounces / 1/4 cup) unsalted butter*
* *1 cup vanilla yogurt (can be low-fat or nonfat)*

Irene's Cranberry Scones

THIS TRADITIONAL BRITISH PASTRY IS MOST OFTEN SERVED
WITH BREAKFAST OR TEA. OFFER THEM TO GUESTS AT ROOM
TEMPERATURE OR SLIGHTLY WARMED, WITH BUTTER AND
PRESERVES FOR SPREADING. *Makes about 12 scones*

1. Preheat oven to 425°F. Grease a baking sheet and
   set aside.

2. In a large bowl, sift together flour, sugar, baking powder,
   and salt.

3. Cut butter into small pieces and cut into flour mixture
   using pastry cutter or two knives; blend until pieces are
   like coarse cornmeal.

4. Add egg and about half of the milk; stir until no flour is
   visible. Add more milk in small amounts if necessary.

5. Add orange zest and cranberries to flour mixture and
   stir to incorporate.

6. Turn dough out onto floured surface; knead gently
   about 15 times; add flour to surface as needed to prevent
   sticking. Cut dough in half. Shape each into a ball, then
   press into $1/2$-inch-thick rounds; and cut into 6 to 8 pie-
   shaped wedges. Glaze tops with beaten egg, if desired.

7. Place wedges on prepared cookie sheet, leaving enough
   space between them so sides do not touch. Bake until
   golden brown, about 10 to 12 minutes.

8. Serve immediately.

* 2 cups sifted
  all-purpose flour, plus
  more for dusting

* 2 tablespoons sugar

* 3 teaspoons
  baking powder

* $1/2$ teaspoon salt

* 5 tablespoons
  unsalted butter

* 1 egg, beaten; plus 1 egg,
  beaten, for glazing
  (optional)

* $3/4$ cup milk

* 1 tablespoon freshly
  grated orange zest

* $3/4$ cup dried sweetened
  cranberries

CHOCOLATE CHIP COOKIES

A PLATE OF HOMEMADE COOKIES IS A SURE WAY TO WELCOME ANY GUEST, BUT CHILDREN WILL TAKE SPECIAL COMFORT FROM THIS TREAT. THIS RECIPE MAKES SOFT COOKIES. FOR CRISPER COOKIES, BAKE 2 TO 3 MINUTES LONGER ON EACH TURN.
Makes about 2 dozen cookies

- 2 sticks (8 ounces / 1 cup) unsalted butter
- ¾ cup firmly packed brown sugar
- ¾ cup granulated sugar
- 3 teaspoons pure vanilla extract
- 2 eggs
- 2¼ cups all-purpose flour
- 1 teaspoon baking soda
- 3 teaspoons salt
- 12 ounces chocolate chips

1. Preheat oven to 375°F.

2. In a large mixing bowl (or in the bowl of an electric mixer), beat together the butter, sugars, and vanilla until creamy.

3. Add the eggs, one at a time, mixing well after each addition.

4. With the mixer still running, gradually add the flour, baking soda, and salt.

5. Add the chocolate chips and mix until all ingredients are well blended.

6. Using a cookie scoop or rounded tablespoon, place mounds on ungreased cookie sheets, approximately 12 per sheet.

7. Bake 1 sheet at a time. Bake 5 minutes, rotate sheet 180 degrees, then bake another 5 minutes.

8. Remove sheet from oven and let sit 2 to 3 minutes. Transfer cookies to wire racks to cool several minutes more.

9. Serve immediately or store in an airtight container at room temperature.

STRAWBERRY ICED TEA

- *2 quarts hot black tea*
- *1/3 to 2/3 cup superfine sugar*
- *1/4 to 1/2 cup freshly squeezed lemon juice*
- *2 pints fresh strawberries, washed and hulled*

Sweeten with Simple Sugar, if desired (recipe follows)

IF MAKING THIS RECIPE IN ADVANCE, MAKE EXTRA TEA AND FREEZE IN ICE CUBE TRAYS. THEN, WHEN THE ICE CUBES MELT IN PITCHER OR GLASSES, THE FLAVOR WILL NOT BE WATERED DOWN. *Makes about 2 quarts*

1. Place tea in a glass mixing bowl. While the tea is still hot, add 1/3 cup sugar and 1/4 cup lemon juice. Stir until sugar has completely dissolved. Taste and add more sugar and lemon juice, as needed. Let cool.

2. Set aside enough berries for garnish and slice them; puree remaining berries.

3. Place puree in a fine-mesh strainer over a pitcher and press pulp through with a wooden spoon.

4. Add cooled tea mixture to pitcher. Chill until ready to serve.

5. Serve over ice with a strawberry slice as a garnish.

Simple Sugar

Since granulated sugar added to iced tea does not dissolve properly, offer guests a sugar syrup instead to sweeten their drink with. Simmer 2 parts water to 1 part sugar over low heat until sugar has dissolved and mixture is clear, boil it for 1 to 2 minutes, then remove from heat and let cool. It will keep refrigerated for 2 to 3 days.

MINT ICED TEA

MINT, DATING BACK TO ANCIENT GREECE, HAS LONG BEEN A SYMBOL OF HOSPITALITY AND MAKES A DELICIOUS COMPLEMENT TO EVERYTHING FROM SIMPLE SANDWICHES TO SOPHISTICATED SALADS. *Makes about 2 quarts*

1. Place tea in a glass mixing bowl. While the tea is still hot, add $1/3$ cup sugar. Stir until sugar has completely dissolved. Taste and add more sugar, as needed. Let cool.

2. Pour tea mixture into a pitcher and chill until ready to serve.

3. Serve over ice with a mint sprig garnish.

* *2 quarts hot black tea, steeped with $1^1/_2$ teaspoons dried mint leaves*

* *$1/_3$ to $2/_3$ cup superfine sugar*

* *mint sprigs, for garnish*

Sweeten with Simple Sugar, if desired (facing page)

Pat's Ginger Iced Tea

When choosing ginger (which, for this recipe, must be fresh, not dried or ground), look for young ginger, since it doesn't need to be peeled. More mature gingerroot has to be delicately peeled — stay away from skin that is wrinkled, since this indicates that the root is dried out. *Makes about 2 quarts*

1. In a medium saucepan, combine ginger and water and bring to a boil. Reduce heat and let simmer for about 10 minutes. Remove from heat and let steep for about 10 minutes.

2. Taste ginger tea to be sure it is strong enough (if it is too strong, dilute with more water).

3. While tea is still warm, stir in sugar to taste until it dissolves. Let cool.

4. Pour into a pitcher and chill until ready to serve.

5. Serve over ice.

* 4 medium pieces ginger root, peeled if necessary and sliced

* 2 quarts filtered water, or more as needed

* Superfine sugar, to taste

Sweeten with Simple Sugar, if desired (page 82)

Hot Chocolate

THIS RECIPE CAN BE MADE AHEAD AND REFRIGERATED,
THEN SIMMERED ON THE STOVE TOP TO REHEAT.
Makes about 4 cups

- 6 tablespoons best-quality unsweetened cocoa powder

- 6 tablespoons sugar

- Dash of salt

- 2 1/2 cups milk

- 2 1/2 cups half-and-half

- 1 teaspoon pure vanilla extract

- Whipped cream, for garnish (optional)

- Peppermint sticks, for stirring (optional)

1. In a saucepan, combine cocoa, sugar, and salt. Slowly add milk to pan. Warm over low heat, stirring until salt and sugar dissolve completely.

2. Add half-and-half and vanilla to pan. Heat until just ready to boil, then remove from heat.

3. Stir and pour into a thermos or other warm-liquid container, or serve immediately.

4. If you wish, top with whipped cream. Add peppermint stick to each mug, if using — as it melts, it will infuse the chocolate with mint flavor.

Activities

Guests will consider your home their base and the local town, nearby areas, events, and sites a playground of sorts. Some may have ideas of what they would like to do, others may leave plans up to you. Don't feel you have to be a cruise director, with something fun scheduled every moment and a slew of surprises around every corner, but do give it a little thought and ask guests before they arrive if there is something in particular they are looking forward to, as some events will require reservations. Don't count out spontaneity, however—spur-of-the-moment decisions can turn out to be the best of all. You want to allow for free time as well— a much-appreciated and often-overlooked detail. For some guests, an all-consuming schedule may make a getaway feel no different than the rigors of their daily lives.

Determine how much or how little activity guests desire and plan accordingly. If you've got a bunch of relatives making camp at your house for a family reunion, there may already be a plethora of festivities, and down time at home is exactly what's called for. If faraway friends are in town for just a weekend and don't plan to return soon, hit the local highlights. Assemble copies of area road maps, local museum and theater schedules, and a selection of literature from other area highlights. Try to include items that range in interest and for varying age levels, like what's happening at a nearby amusement park and what plays, musicians, and movies are in town. Or plan just one main outing over the weekend, leaving a free schedule and plenty of time to take leisurely strolls and catch up with family and old friends.

Sporting Equipment Checklists

Remind guests what they will need before they arrive so they can pack what's necessary or be prepared to rent equipment. Here are sample checklists for three sports.

Skiing and Snowboarding

- *Skis or snowboard and bindings*
- *Boots*
- *Poles*
- *Helmet*
- *Ski pants*
- *Earmuffs/headband*
- *Gloves*
- *Jacket*
- *Thermals*
- *Socks*
- *Goggles/sunglasses*
- *Ski rack for car*
- *Sunblock*
- *Lip balm*
- *Pack or bag*
- *Wax*
- *Cell phone*

Boating and Canoeing

- *Boat shoes or sandals*
- *Windbreaker*
- *Visor/hat*
- *Water socks (if you jump into shallow water)*
- *Sunglasses*
- *Sunblock*
- *Lip balm*
- *Towels*
- *Change of clothes in waterproof container*
- *Long pants, long sleeves, blanket for after sunset*
- *Life preserver (if boat will not be equipped with them)*
- *Waterproof camera*
- *Binoculars*
- *Snorkels and masks, diving equipment*
- *Waterproof container for wallet, etc.*

Keep a message board in the kitchen: on it you can leave notes for guests about schedules, weather, and ideas. A chalkboard makes for easy cleanup and reuse; you can also use a ribbon board or good, old-fashioned corkboard for hanging printed material or your own notes. Leave extra keys hanging on another board — paint a piece of wood or cover a surface with canvas — and hang this one by the front or back door so guests can come and go as they please. By each hook, mark FRONT DOOR, EQUIPMENT SHED, BIKE LOCKS, and such.

If you are making the plans, let guests' interests and the area's local flavor guide you. You'll find different activities for your best friend who loves live music or a studious niece who's into architecture. Consider the reason for the get-together, the season, the time of day, the location. Then let your activity guide the preparation, the schedule, even some meals. Following are a few sample itineraries to inspire and guide you. Choose points of each you like and think of them broadly so you can put them to use for whatever you decide to do.

Day Trip to Sporting/Recreation Area

If you've got an athletic crowd coming to stay and you live in an area that's good for sports (whether skiing, boating, biking, climbing, fishing, hiking, etc.) devote a day to one sport or recreation area. Scope out nearby facilities, locations, and accommodations first. Be sure to get all the pertinent information, such as days and hours of operation, expected conditions, prices for tickets or equipment rentals, and restaurants or rest areas.

Hiking

- *Hiking shoes or boots*
- *Tall socks with wicking ability*
- *Long-sleeved shirt*
- *Basic first-aid kit*
- *Hat*
- *Gloves*
- *Fleece pullover*
- *Snacks*
- *Backpack or fanny pack*
- *Map*
- *Camera*
- *Binoculars*
- *Matches*
- *Garbage bags*
- *Emergency marker*
- *Flashlight*
- *Bandana*
- *Cell phone/walkie-talkie*
- *Multifunctional pocket knife*
- *Sunglasses*
- *Sunblock*
- *Lip balm*
- *Bug spray*
- *Water bottle, water purifier*
- *Loud whistle*

When your cousins from Florida are coming in and you know they look forward to skiing, pencil in plenty of slope time. This is a day that will start early and end late, so there is lots of planning to be done. Call around to the nearest ski areas about a week before your relatives are due to arrive. Ask about expected conditions, travel time, prices for lift tickets, equipment rentals, lessons—a group lesson for novices or those who need a bit of brushing up might be a fun idea. Any of these expenses are hefty enough that you should not expect to pay: send info (including prices) to guests in advance. See what equipment you have for yourself and others and make sure it's in tip-top shape. The same legwork will be necessary for a day of hiking, canoeing, or other sport.

To make the most of any sport-filled day, you'll want to get up and out early in the morning, so have everyone pack up the night before. Set out outerwear and accessories so they are ready to go. For skiing or any activity like boating, set out a big duffel bag for everyone to throw in a dry change of clothes, then toss it in the back of the car. Stock the car with extra drinking water, a first-aid kit, snack bars, and, in winter, a few blankets (don't take these until the morning so they'll still be warm from indoors). Just before you leave, line up a few pairs of cozy slippers by the front door—this small gesture will be the ultimate in comfort at the end of a tiring day and much appreciated.

Be ready with a quick, light breakfast like scones and muffins, along with thermoses of hot tea, coffee, or hot chocolate for the ride. If possible, plan to eat lunch out—a restaurant can be a good destination for cyclist or even urban hikers. For a boat, beach, or otherwise restricted outing, you'll want to pack easy-to-make foods like sandwiches, chips, and sodas. Then, have a no-nonsense dinner planned at home—on cold days, think warm comfort food like already prepared soup with a loaf of crusty bread, or a big bowl of pasta and sauce with a tossed side salad. Warm nights call for premade burger patties, chicken, or steaks grilled on the barbeque.

Details and Information

When you have decided on a sports activity, have this information ready for guests:

- Directions and map to sporting area (and home), if you will be taking more than one car

- Phone numbers of local areas if guests want to scope out more than one

- A list of nearby attractions or shopping spots for nonsporters who want to tag along to the area but not participate in the sport

- Cell phone numbers of group members if you will be splitting up, plus any necessary emergency numbers

- Expected snow, water, and weather conditions

FELT CAMERA COVER

EVEN THE MOST BASIC ITEMS, SUCH AS DISPOSABLE
CAMERAS, CAN BE WRAPPED IN PRETTY PACKAGING TO
MAKE THEM SEEM SPECIAL. HERE, A BUTTON IS USED AS
A DECORATIVE FASTENER, BUT YOU CAN USE ANYTHING
YOU LIKE — SUCH AS APPLIQUÉD FLOWERS, RIBBONS,
OR OTHER NOTIONS.

You will need:

ruler, disposable camera, fabric pencil, felt or other fabric, pinking shears or scallop-edged scissors, needle, thread, button or other fastener

1. With ruler, measure front (height), back (height), top (width), and bottom (width) of camera; add together. Then measure length of the camera, along front side. With fabric pencil, mark off rectangle on fabric that is 5 inches longer than first measurement and $3^1/_2$ inches longer than the second.

2. Cut out rectangle using pinking shears, allowing a 1-inch give on top and bottom and both sides so final rectangle will be 3 inches by $1^1/_2$ inches longer than original measurement.

3. Place camera on fabric; position it so it is centered on length (with a $^3/_4$-inch overhang on each side) and so that top flap overlaps bottom flap (on front side) about $1^1/_2$ inches down from top edge.

4. Sew on button, tacking top and bottom flaps to secure.

SPICED CIDER

THIS RECIPE IS GOOD YEAR-ROUND — SERVE HOT DURING CHILLY MONTHS AND COLD DURING WARMER WEATHER OVER ICE. *Makes about 2 quarts*

* 2 quarts apple cider
* 2 tablespoons light brown sugar
* 1 teaspoon whole cloves, plus more for garnish
* 1 teaspoon whole allspice berries
* 2 cinnamon sticks
* Pinch of salt
* 6 to 8 lemon slices, plus more for garnish

1. Combine all ingredients in large saucepan and warm over medium heat, stirring until sugar dissolves.

2. Bring to a boil, then reduce heat to simmer. Cover and simmer for 15 minutes.

3. Strain. Serve immediately if drinking hot. Otherwise, let cool and then refrigerate.

4. For garnish, stud lemon slices with cloves, and float on top of each serving.

The Perfect Pasta Sauce

AT THE END OF A BUSY DAY SKIING, SIGHTSEEING,
OR SHOPPING, COME HOME TO A HEARTY DINNER THAT
YOU'VE PREPARED IN ADVANCE. PAIR THIS ALL-PURPOSE
SAUCE WITH YOUR FAVORITE PASTA AND SPINACH
SALAD (PAGE 99) FOR A SATISFYING MEAL THAT'S
READY IN MINUTES. *Makes 4 cups*

1. Pour ¼ inch olive oil into the bottom of a large
   stockpot and warm over medium heat.

2. Add onion and garlic to oil and sauté until very
   lightly browned.

3. Add salt and pepper to taste and sauté
   1 to 2 minutes more.

4. Add tomatoes and tomato paste; stir well, mashing
   whole tomatoes against side of pot to break up.

5. Add oregano and basil; stir well.

6. Cover and let simmer for 1 to 2 hours,
   stirring occasionally.

* *Olive oil*
* *1 large onion, sliced*
* *2 cloves garlic,
  peeled and minced*
* *Salt and freshly ground
  black pepper, to taste*
* *One 28-ounce can whole
  tomatoes with basil leaf*
* *One 8-ounce can
  tomato paste*
* *¼ teaspoon
  dried oregano*
* *½ teaspoon dried basil*

*Prepare this sauce up to
two weeks in advance and
freeze — take out to defrost
before you leave for the day
or refrigerate a couple of
days beforehand.*

SPINACH SALAD

SPEND MORE TIME WITH FRIENDS AND LESS TIME IN THE
KITCHEN WHEN YOU SERVE THIS SIMPLE BUT DELICIOUS
SALAD. PREPARE THE INGREDIENTS AHEAD OF TIME, THEN
STORE IN SEPARATE CONTAINERS IN THE REFRIGERATOR
UNTIL READY TO USE. THE DRESSING CAN ALSO BE MADE
IN ADVANCE AND REFRIGERATED. *Makes 4 to 6 servings*

1. Combine salad ingredients in large salad bowl and
   toss to mix.

2. Combine dressing ingredients in jar and shake well.
   Just before serving, pour dressing over salad and mix
   thoroughly, making sure to coat all spinach leaves.

For the salad:

* *1 bunch or 16-ounce
  package fresh spinach,
  washed thoroughly and
  patted dry*

* *8 large mushrooms,
  cleaned and sliced*

* *1 can mandarin oranges,
  drained and rinsed*

* *1 ripe avocado,
  thinly sliced*

For the dressing:

* *1/2 cup olive oil*

* *1/4 cup apple cider vinegar*

* *1/4 cup sugar*

* *1/2 teaspoon salt*

* *1/2 teaspoon paprika*

* *1/4 teaspoon dry mustard*

* *1/8 teaspoon freshly
  ground black pepper*

* *1/2 white onion,
  finely chopped*

Day Trip Checklist

- *Binoculars*
- *Comfortable walking shoes*
- *Layered clothing, for changes in weather*
- *Strollers (sometimes they can be rented)*
- *Backpack*
- *Snacks*
- *Bottled water*
- *Camera and film*
- *Sketch pad and pencils*
- *Money for admission, parking, souvenirs*
- *Picnic basket (see checklist on page 103)*

Day Trip to Local Attraction

An outing to a museum, botanical garden, or historic site can be fun for grown-ups and children alike, since there will likely be interesting exhibits for parents and special programs for the kids. When you truly want to center your day around children, plan a half or full day at the zoo, amusement park, science center, or other kid-oriented venue. Families, singles, and couples can stay with the group or venture out to explore on their own.

It's important to be flexible, rather than setting rules or limits. Let others know that this day is about "want-tos" rather than "have-tos." Consider everyone's physical and mental limits: Kids can get overtired or bored quickly, and older folks may not be able to handle loud music or long walks. Breaking for lunch is always a good idea. If you will be separating, make a plan as to where and when to meet up — ideally an easy-to-find restaurant or someplace relatively close to where you parked in order to grab the picnic lunch you prepared from the trunk.

If you are bringing lunch, pack quick and simple fare and bring a blanket or two to lay down on the grass in case no picnic tables are available. Sandwiches for the grown-ups — like grilled vegetables with balsamic vinegar on peasant bread, cucumbers and goat cheese, or grilled chicken with smoked mozzarella and sun-dried tomatoes — all taste delicious at room temperature. If you don't have time to make them, stop at a sandwich shop and choose a variety. Kids tend to like their sandwiches a bit less gourmet. Peanut butter and jelly, American or Swiss cheese, even a variety of cold cuts will be a big hit—especially if you cut them into fanciful shapes using cookie cutters. Take a stylish approach to utensils: Roll them in paper napkins and tie with a decorative ribbon. A bottle of wine will add a festive note to the gathering (bring bottled water, too); for children, bring juice or soda bottles with straws. To round out the meal, add macaroni salad (see page 105) or potato salad (see page 104), chips, fruit, and homemade cookies for dessert (see page 80).

Call ahead to the location to inquire about hours of operation, parking rules, special exhibits or performances, child-related programs, and admission charges. If you are coming with a large crowd, you might qualify for group deals; if you are a member of a related society, ask about discounts. Your guests' admission fees are not your responsibility, although if they are nominal, you might want to pay. Alternatively, guests may take this opportunity to treat you and your family. Again, it's a good idea to give guests all the information ahead of time. That way people can have time to decide if they would like to join in or not.

PICNIC BASKET
CHECKLIST

⬧ Blanket(s) ⬧

⬧ Plates ⬧

⬧ Utensils and serving pieces ⬧

⬧ Plastic cups / glasses (wine and water) ⬧

⬧ Napkins ⬧

⬧ Placemats or tablecloth for
picnic table ⬧

⬧ Corkscrew ⬧

⬧ Knife and cheese slicer ⬧

⬧ Weights to hold blanket down ⬧

⬧ Food, wrapped or packaged well ⬧

⬧ Beverages
(in a separate cooler, if necessary) ⬧

⬧ Bottled water ⬧

⬧ Bud vase with flower
(to add a special note) ⬧

Irene's Garlic Pickle
Potato Salad

THE PICKLES ADD A BIT OF CRUNCH TO THIS SALAD,
THE PICKLE JUICE A LITTLE TANGINESS. BOTH INGREDIENT
AMOUNTS CAN BE ADJUSTED TO TASTE OR LEFT
OUT COMPLETELY. *Makes 6 servings*

* 3 pounds russet potatoes

* 6 tablespoons store-bought mayonnaise, plus more to taste

* 1 tablespoon milk

* ¼ cup pickle juice (optional)

* 1 teaspoon Dijon mustard, plus more to taste

* 3 kosher-style garlic pickles, diced (or any pickle style you desire; optional)

* 4 hard-boiled eggs, diced

1. In a large pot, boil potatoes in water until fork soft. Peel and dice into $\frac{1}{2}$-inch cubes (or slice if preferred).

2. In a large bowl, combine mayonnaise, milk, pickle juice, if using, and mustard; whisk until consistency is creamy.

3. Add potatoes to mayonnaise mixture and mix; add pickles, if using, and eggs and mix well.

4. Refrigerate overnight, if possible, or at least 3 hours. Add more mayonnaise before serving, if necessary.

Iris's Crunchy Macaroni Salad

THIS VERSATILE DISH IS FAVORITE PICNIC AND
BARBECUE FARE. IT STORES WELL IN THE REFRIGERATOR
AND IS WONDERFUL A DAY OR TWO LATER AS A LEFTOVER
SIDE DISH. *Make 6 servings*

1. Cook macaroni, following directions on package.
   Drain, then run under cold water.

2. Add oil and stir to coat pasta.

3. Add all remaining ingredients except mayonnaise
   and mix well.

4. Mix in mayonnaise to taste.

- One 15-ounce package
  small elbow macaroni

- 2 tablespoons olive oil

- 3 tablespoons
  minced celery

- 1 tablespoon
  minced onion

- $1/2$ cup grated sharp
  cheddar cheese

- 2 to 3 tablespoons
  prepared mayonnaise,
  or to taste

Sightseeing

Part of the fun of entertaining guests is introducing them to what is special in your area, especially for those folks from out of town. What is your town famous for? What constitutes the local flavor? What are some quirky or unusual sights? What are the regional cuisines?

When mapping out a day of sightseeing, have a strategy in mind. Otherwise you might go full steam ahead and find that the group loses momentum or interest halfway through. Don't plan big trips back to back on the same day — after tramping around on the waterfront, it's better to leave out the trip to the aquarium in favor of lunch at the seafood restaurant down the street. Plan high-energy activities for the morning, when people are their freshest. If you will be doing a lot of walking, make sure there are plenty of spots to sit down and rest along the way. If you will be going all day, schedule a snack or beverage break between lunch and dinner.

Going antiquing and combing flea markets are wonderful ways to show guests the area's art, history, traditions, and personalities — and the best part is that they can bring some treasures home. Don't hesitate to take guests down that old country road to find your favorite spot — look to see if any roadside stands or the bakehouse are open and hit them for lunch on the way back. You always want to be prepared when you come across that perfect find: advise everyone to bring plenty of cash (or checks), totes for purchases, swatches to match up potential purchases, and cell phones to keep in touch.

After a day spent going here and there, why not top it off with dinner at a restaurant that will make a lasting impression? Many areas are well known for their culinary specialties—and many restaurants for their atmosphere. If there is a view of the sun setting over the water, ask for a table next to the window. If it's pure magic on a verandah overlooking a vineyard, book a table out there. If you'll be dining in a large restaurant filled with hustle and bustle, gauge if guests want to be in the center of it all, then ask to be seated in such a place; if a more intimate setting is likely to please, find out about a quieter spot or perhaps a private room. Small family-owned establishments often offer extra-special attention. Make reservations, especially if you are bringing a large group.

MAKING DINNER RESERVATIONS

What to tell/ask when you call for reservations:

- *If you have someone in your party celebrating a special occasion*

- *That you will be paying—ask how to prearrange this*

- *If you have guests with special dietary restrictions*

- *If you have children in your party who will require booster seats or high chairs*

- *If there is a smoking section*

- *If liquor is served or if you can bring your own*

- *If you can see a copy of the wine list (to preorder wine)*

- *What the daily specials will be, if there are any specialty dishes that require at least 24 hours' notice.*

- *If there is a dress code*

- *If there is any on-site entertainment*

Staying Home

There are some days and nights that call for just a crowd gathered around a table playing games or sprawled in the living room watching a movie, chatting, or listening to music. Whatever you do, you'll value the quality time spent together. Organize a game night and it might last well into the early morning as guests eat, drink, laugh, and play. Food can be quite casual and fun. Serve unfussy hors d'oeuvres, sliced vegetables, chips, and dips, or something more elaborate, like fondue. In the evening, make s'mores by the fire or in the kitchen. Mix drinks at the bar and offer nonalcoholic refreshments as well, both hot and cold, like sodas, iced teas (see pages 82–85), cider (see page 96) and hot chocolate (see page 86).

Have a selection of music in several genres on hand so you can be certain to play something guests will like. If there are no requests, pick music you enjoy that will fit the mood. For a group, it's also a good idea to have a selection of games that can be played together.

Popular Games

- *Backgammon*
- *Dominoes*
- *Cards (supply multiple decks) and poker chips*
- *Checkers*
- *Chess*
- *Chinese checkers*
- *Monopoly*
- *Scrabble*

- *Guacamole, salsa, and chips*

- *Shrimp with cocktail sauce*

- *Hummus and baba ghanoush with pita bread triangles and fresh vegetables*

- *Warmed brie topped with sliced almonds and served with melba rounds*

- *Bruschetta topped with diced tomatoes or olive tapenade*

- *Cheese or chocolate fondue*

- *Platter of cheeses, served with crackers or French bread*

- *Buffalo chicken wings with blue cheese dipping sauce and celery stalks*

- *Fresh fruit skewers dusted with powdered sugar or served with creamy yogurt dip*

- *Local specialties: smoked salmon in the Northwest, mini-chicken quesadillas in the Southwest, fried green tomatoes in the South, etc.*

EASY PICKUP GAMES — THAT ANYBODY CAN PLAY

What's fun about these games is that there's no need for gameboards, equipment, or formal planning and organization. Many have been played for decades and continue to provide a good time for all.

Charades

Everyone in the group is handed slips of paper to write the name of a person, title, or character from well-known fields such as television, books, movies, or politics. The group divides into two teams. Alternating teams on each turn, one person chooses a slip of paper and stands before the group, attempting to describe the name on the paper to the other players on her team using only hand movements and gestures — no talking allowed. Except, of course, from the raucous crowd trying to figure out the clues! The team with the most correct guesses wins.

Twenty Questions

An old favorite guessing game, this one allows only the categories "animal," "vegetable," and "mineral" as clues. Someone in the group thinks of an "answer" and the other players are allowed to ask up to twenty questions to find out just what the item is. Questions have to be phrased so that answers are only "yes," or "no," or "I don't know."

The Name Game

This is a great game to play with a group that is meeting for the first time. Cut sheets of paper into short strips that are long enough to write a person or character's first and last names. Give each player ten or so strips, let them write names (can be from modern times or history, a real person or a character from a book, play, movie, and so on — it just has to be someone whose name most people will recognize). Players fold strips in half, then add to a communal bowl. One person mixes up the names and pins or tapes a strip to each person's back. The players then mingle and ask one another questions about their "name," and the first person to guess correctly is the winner. Be sure not to play this game in a room with a large mirror!

Word Association

One player at a time thinks of a word, then the next player has to think of (and say) a word that is somehow related (the relation can be rather remote!). After everyone has had a turn, try to guess at what the connections are between the seemingly random words. It is quite fun to see where the line starts and finishes — usually in too much laughter to continue!

Geography Game

This is a fun game for kids. The starting player names a place anywhere in the world (can be a continent, country, state, province, county, or city); the next player needs to think of a place that begins with the last letter of the previously stated place, and so on.

Peanut Butter S'mores

CLASSIC S'MORES ARE THE PERFECT SNACK FOR A COZY NIGHT AT HOME, SINCE ROASTING THE MARSHMALLOWS TOGETHER IS DELIGHTFUL FUN FOR YOU AND YOUR GUESTS. CREAMY PEANUT BUTTER CHIPS ADD EXTRA DECADENCE TO THESE TIME-HONORED TREATS BUT CAN BE LEFT OUT FOR THE TRADITIONALISTS IN THE CROWD. *Serves 2*

1. On a plate, place graham crackers side by side.

2. On one cracker, place chocolate pieces, enough to cover face of cracker, leaving a small border.

3. Sprinkle peanut butter chips over chocolate.

4. Carefully roast marshmallows over fire in fireplace or on stove top, until marshmallows are a toasted brown color.

5. Gently slide hot marshmallows onto graham cracker covered with chocolate and peanut butter chips; top with other cracker to make sandwich and press down gently.

- *2 large graham crackers*
- *Good-quality chocolate, broken into chunks or shaved*
- *1 tablespoon peanut butter chips*
- *2 marshmallows*

Saying Good-bye

The final moments of a visit can come too quickly and be filled with mixed emotions. There is excitement for the time spent together and sadness that it is coming to an end. There are promises to call and to send pictures and to see each other again soon. Early flights and long road trips often have guests setting out first thing in the morning or just after breakfast. Some may have the luxury of staying though lunch, prolonging their visit a few hours more.

No matter what time they leave, don't let guests go empty-handed. Give everyone a special token as a reminder of their stay. A local treat is always appreciated, such as a bottle of maple syrup from a local New England farm, a bottle of good Northwest or California wine, or a package of Southwest specialty spices. Other ideas: attach a wooden honey swizzle stick to a jar of the golden nectar with raffia or tie a few herb sachets (see page 48) together with ribbon.

And don't send guests off without something to eat. Pack breakfast for those who will be off early and make sure everyone gets a snack to go: fill a wood or metal box with spiced nuts, dried fruit, pretzels, chips, and other easy-to-munch treats. Bottled water will also be much appreciated. As you wave so long, don't be surprised if you're already thinking about the next get-together. After all, you've got a wonderful home, wonderful friends and family, and, now, the wonderful ways of a gracious host.

Resources

**Home Accessories
and Tableware**

Conran Shop
 Bridgemarket
 407 East 59th Street
 New York, NY 10022
 212-755-9079

 Michelin House
 81 Fulham Road
 London, England SW3
 020.7589.7401
 www.conran.com

Crate & Barrel
 800.967.6696
 www.crateandbarrel.com
 call for store locations
  or catalog

Gracious Home
 800-338-7809
 www.gracioushome.com
 call for store locations

IKEA
 800.434.4532
 www.ikea.com
 call for store locations
  or catalog

John Lewis Partnership
 278-306 Oxford Street
 London, England W1A
 020.7629.7711

Pottery Barn
 800.588.6250
 www.potterybarn.com
 call for store locations
  or catalog

Restoration Hardware
 800.762.1005
 www.restorationhardware.com
 call for store locations
  or catalog

Williams-Sonoma
 800.541.2233
 www.williams-sonoma.com
 call for store locations
  or catalog

Z Gallerie
 800.385.8288
 www.zgallerie.com
 call for store locations

**Towels, Bath Accessories,
and Fixtures**

Bath & Body Works
   800.518.3616
   www.bathandbodyworks.com
   call for store locations

Cost Plus World Market
   www.costplus.com
   search for store locations
      online

Waterworks
   800.998.2284
   www.waterworks.com
   call for store locations
      or catalog

Bed Linens and Accessories

Garnet Hill
   800.870.3513
   www.garnethill.com
   call for catalog

Hable Construction Inc.
   230 Elizabeth Street
   New York, NY 10012
   212.343.8555
   www.hableconstruction.com

Target
   800.800.8800
   www.target.com
   call for store locations

INDEX

Planning and Preparations

Table of Equivalents

Liquid/Dry Measures

U.S.		METRIC		U.S.		METRIC	
$1/4$	teaspoon	1.25	milliliters	$1/8$	inch	3	millimeters
$1/2$	teaspoon	2.5	milliliters	$1/4$	inch	6	millimeters
1	teaspoon	5	milliliters	$1/2$	inch	12	millimeters
1	tablespoon (3 teaspoons)	15	milliliters	1	inch	2.5	centimeters
1	fluid ounce (2 tablespoons)	30	milliliters				
$1/4$	cup	60	milliliters				
$1/3$	cup	80	milliliters				
$1/2$	cup	120	milliliters				
1	cup	240	milliliters				
1	pint (2 cups)	480	milliliters				
1	quart (4 cups, 32 ounces)	960	milliliters				
1	gallon (4 quarts)	3.84	liters				
1	ounce (by weight)	28	grams				
1	pound	454	grams				
2.2	pounds	1	kilogram				

OVEN TEMPERATURE

FAHRENHEIT	CELSIUS	GAS
250	120	$1/2$
275	140	1
300	150	2
325	160	3
350	180	4
375	190	5
400	200	6
425	220	7
450	230	8
475	240	9
500	260	10